I Made It, and So Can You!

Triumphing Over the Rough Stuff in Life

Xaviar Jackson

Copyright © 2020 by Xaviar Jackson

All rights reserved

Although the author and publisher have exhaustively researched sources to ensure the accuracy and completeness of the information contained in this book, we assume no responsibility for errors, inaccuracies, omissions, or any other inconsistency herein. Some names have been changed to protect privacy. Any slights against people or organizations are unintentional.

ISBN: 978-1-948638-12-8 (softcover)

Published by

Fideli Publishing, Inc.
119 W. Morgan St.
Martinsville, IN 46151

www.FideliPublishing.com

MANUFACTURED IN THE UNITED STATES OF AMERICA

Dedicated to

Willie L. Grayson
6/13/1955-10/052011

I Made It, and So Can You!

Triumphing Over the Rough Stuff in Life

Table of Contents

A Note from the Author ix
Don't Follow the Crowd Be a Leader............ 1
Things Are Not Always What They Seem..... 3
What Would God Have You Do? 7
Trust in God, Not Man 11
All in God's Time 15
Learning Servitude 17
Keys to Success 19
Choices Carry Consequences...................... 21
Let It Go... 23
In His time... 25
Finding Contentment................................. 27
God Will Provide 29
Everything He Does is on Time.................. 33
Never give up... 35
Final Words from the Author 37

Whatever it is that you do so well,
it's not for you to be lifted up in self-glory.
He's graced you to do that particular thing
so give honor back to Him.

A Note from the Author

This book is intended to tell some of my most valuable moments in time. I openly invite you into a part of my life that was very sensitive, yet needed to make me who I've become today. The ups and downs helped me to become who I am at this very moment.

To whoever reads this, may everything your hands touch thrive and prosper. Be great in every aspect you so desire, because YOU are worth it! May you be inspired, motivated, and rise above every obstacle that comes your way. You know why? Because only YOU can stand in your own way. I've found out that the road to success is never-ending.

I'm Xaviar Davon Jackson, a 20-year-old male who grew up in the small town of Demopolis, Alabama. When I was younger, I was full of energy. I came from a family that didn't have much, but I never lacked in any area. My mother and grandmother were two hardworking women who provided for me the best they could. All of our days weren't golden, but with the help of God, we've made it this far.

I can honestly say, as a child from a single parent home, I didn't turn out all that bad. I often questioned myself; wondering if I were doing things right. I soon realized I didn't have to have it all together right away, but I did have to be willing to make a continual effort toward that goal.

I don't take credit for anything I have done over the course of my life, because if it were not for the Man above, I would not be where I am today.

As a young person, you long to be recognized and appreciated for what you do. It's a need for the personal satisfaction of making a difference in this cold, criticizing world. Life's experiences will make you question if what you're doing is actually worth it. Well, it really is.

Quite a few of our parents worked typical 9-5 jobs, and hammered into us the importance of respect and good moral character. What seemed to be a boring, repetitive cycle of never-ending Monday through Friday drudgery made us quickly realize that in order to make it you HAD to have these two characteristics. As you mature, you come to realize that your parents only wanted you to be better people in every way possible.

Understand that the greatest achievement is to just be YOU. That may sound simple, but has a lot of meaning.

There won't always be clean-cut victories,
sometimes the victory
is found within the victor.

Don't Follow the Crowd
Be a Leader

By the time I was 11 years old, I'd obtained a basic understanding of the things of God, and I knew I was different. Many young people think it's strange to find no interest in what others consider the norm. What I quickly learned was that it's okay to be a leader, rather than following the crowd. I understood that it's better to have a passion for a particular thing or idea than to just do something for popularity's sake any day.

Have you ever wondered about that uneasy feeling you have in certain situations, or that tug on your heart when you're around the wrong group of people? That's the Holy Spirit nudging you in a different direction, in order to protect you from the dangers you can't see.

Living a saved life *does not* mean you can't still have fun. Life won't always be easy or fair, but He will make the journey worth holding on to. Prayer, faith, and knowing how to wait on God are all key aspects of my daily advancement in Him.

When I was younger, I never would have thought I'd meet the people I've met or go to the places I have traveled. My process is not yet finished, but I know without a doubt in my mind and heart that I was going to be used greatly to edify the kingdom of God. I also learned that doing this means you will not always be everyone's favorite person, and that's okay because you are the next young person's guiding light.

Things Are Not Always What They Seem

My life changed for what I thought was the worst in 2011. My confidant, my right-hand man, went home to be with the Lord. I was numb for almost a year, struggling to understand why this happened. I began to question God. How could he let someone who was a part of me be taken away? The man had been my number-one motivator and my best friend. Most of all, he was my Grandfather. He taught me everything I needed to know, even the overwhelmingly sad fact of living without him.

Although on an intellectual level I knew death comes to all of us, I was not mentally or emotionally prepared for it when it happened to someone I loved. What I've come to find out is that young people don't take losses too well. We feel as if we're too young for this to happen and wonder why it couldn't happen to someone else. Truth of the matter is, sometimes not so fortunate things happen to good people—even young people.

These things are rough for us individually, but give inspiration for others on a testimonial level. We go through trials and tribulations in life so that others may see that the same God that brought us out of it, is able to deliver them as well. I've learned that we never get over death, we just learn to deal with it.

During my loss, I became depressed and fell short academically while trying to complete my 6th grade year of middle school. It was not until I gathered myself and began an honest effort to come out of that dark hole, that I came back to myself. It was then that I heard a soft voice say to me, *"He's all right."* From that moment on, I began to rejoice, even in the midst of my storm. What I couldn't see at the beginning of this trial was that this was actually a chance for me to become better.

The word of God simply tells us that everything works together for the good of those that love Him and are called according to His purpose (Romans 8:28). For that very reason, I realized I had everything to live for.

Always remember the opposition you're faced with today will come to an end some way, somehow. It's up to you to decide how to approach the Goliath that's in your life. The tears and heartache are all a part of your life's journey and will shape you into the person you're meant to become.

Become known as a fighter as well as someone who endures the everyday trials of life. It is because of what we go through, that we're made better.

You're gonna have to learn that for God to do some things for you fully, you MUST guard those dreams, visions and what He's spoken to you as if your life depends on it!

What Would God Have You Do?

As you know, you must work hard and honestly to reach your goals. We can sometimes plan until we're blue in the face, and all of our goals seem realistic. Some of our planned goals may indeed be "reachable" but is that what our Father in Heaven would have us to do at that moment? Oftentimes, we dive into things prematurely, not fully understanding the foundation of what we're trying to achieve. We can become so overwhelmed with the outside show, that we miss the inside picture. It is not until you fully submit yourself to God that you will understand that *His* timing is what's so precious.

My life has never been a walk in the park. I've encountered a low season of "failed plans." From the time I was a young boy, I dreamed of being a mortician. I worked diligently for what I wanted all through school. I'm a firm believer in "your name will enter rooms, that your feet have yet to enter." This landed me one particular scholarship, just by a simple question being asked of my school secretary, who thought enough of me to recommend me to someone else.

I've learned that people are always watching our lives from afar, and your name has the ability to meet you in unknown places. People don't have to be kind to you, but when they are you should have the decency to thank them. I took this opportunity as serious business, and I hit the ground running. I knew what I was going to college for, and I meant to do just that.

I worked hard through high school to prepare for my life after school. I accumulated over $4,500 in scholarship money towards furthering my education. I was well on my way with move-in day just around the corner. This was an experience I had never encountered and it is one I will never forget. The friends I made there were unforgettable, and I was able to become my own person in a new place.

I enjoyed my new life in a new place for two years. After two semesters, the life I'd carefully built shattered in a matter of seconds. All of my hard work was gone. I was not able to advance to the next semester. I couldn't comprehend what had happened.

This took me so low in spirit, but I pretended I was okay. I felt as if I only had one shot at my dream, and it didn't work. I felt depleted, angry, and hurt to the core; I felt like this was the end.

View the lives of others to be inspired,
not entrapped...

Trust in God, Not Man

What was I going to do? I didn't know anything else to do but weep at the thought of this question. I did not know then why things happened the way they did. A year later, let's be honest, I can see that I put TOTAL trust in man, not God. Because of this, I lost a part of my life I wouldn't be able to get back. I couldn't see it what I had done, and I relied on my own interpretation of events without consulting God first.

Misunderstandings and scandals plagued me, and this all came about because I was trying to reach that goal. My trust was shaky and my perception was blurred. It weighed on me, and it showed everywhere in my life, even simple conversations.

Several months later, I got tired of carrying around the garbage of my life experience. I made a conscious decision to truly let it go and move on. I'd been set free from a prison of my own making that only existed in my mind.

I told God, "It happened, and I can't change it. If and when You bring that season back around to me; it is then when I will move upon it again". I had to pray myself out of a dark place, because the longer I dwelled there, the worse it played on my mind.

As I look back now, I realize I was made stronger by this experience. I had to suffer for God to get the glory. I had to remember that this was divinely appointed to happen to me just the way it did.

I Made It, and So Can You!

I learned that If we don't go through trials in life, we won't truly learn. Anything that comes to us without hassle, won't last long. This process is sometimes painful, but it's well worth it in the end. So free yourself from the time schedule and restrictions you've set for yourself.

Don't base your self-perception upon what someone else considers success. Run *your* race, and do it with patience and trust in God.

After you've suffered awhile, you will find out that He had to allow you to go through those things to establish a sure foundation. What will you be built on when trouble finds you?

All in God's Time

Sure, you can be gifted in a particular way, but if you operate out of season, you are not effective.

I call the moments in life where it seems as if things are not moving a "breezeway." Plans fail, and it's sometimes due to the fact that we didn't acknowledge God first. Just remember this: If you would just wait on God before you make your move, and work diligently with what He's already given you, He will enlarge your territory in due season!

Waiting on anything is indeed a hard thing to do, but it *will* be worth it. Those things that happened to you way back when, or even last year, are helping to build your success. Some of you can clearly "see" the backstory of your success, even when it seemed as if it was a failed attempt. Roadblocks are indeed necessary, they shield you from potential accidents down the road. I was delayed, but God had not denied me of the plans He had for me.

Learning Servitude

My middle school to high school years were the most prominent and profound of my life. I became active in many student-led organizations, and reached a level of relatability among my peers. What I learned early on was the importance of servitude. Serving is one of the most important building blocks of your life.

I served as a member of SGA all four of my high school years, becoming president my final year. Those were big shoes to fill and I had no prior experience. I took my position seriously, knowing that I was setting an example for those who would follow behind me.

Leadership is indeed a great and humbling honor. I often wondered, *Why me?* Why did people choose me to do things when they could've chosen someone else?

Keys to Success

What I want you to understand is you oftentimes don't realize your own hidden potential. It's hidden, which is good for a season. Others sometimes have to help you realize the potential you carry. In this, you are now able to activate those around you.

Mix these ingredients to find success:
- Acknowledge God in all you do.
- Realize that you are God's child and He cares for you.
- Seek Him first and all His righteousness.

- Work diligently toward your destiny.
- Don't be afraid to operate in what He's given you.
- Use your talents and gifts; someone's life could depend on it
- Pray daily.
- Be the best you that you can be.
- Never diminish or devalue who you are just to fit in.
- Constantly evaluate the people and things in your inner circle.
- Live by God's Word.

In today's world, forgiveness is a subject that many don't touch on, because they want to avoid being rubbed the wrong way. No matter how much it hurts, you must forgive.

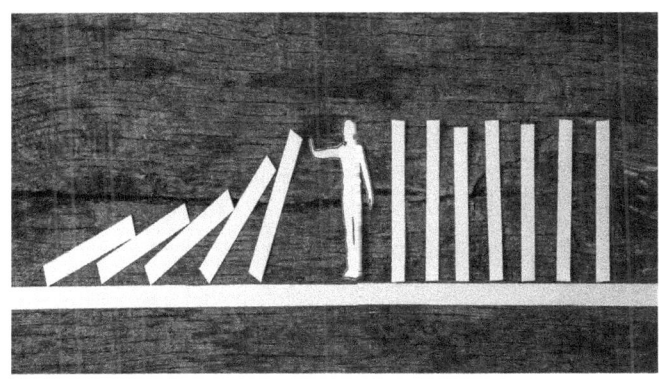

Choices Carry Consequences

I was a young child in a single parent household, and my upbringing was a bit odd sometimes. After my grandpa's passing, there was a void. I missed having a male figure in my home, and all the security and help that came with it. This void grew bigger and bigger. The high school years are so important to kids. My proms, graduations, and school functions all felt lacking because my grandfather wasn't there to share them. There was no one to fill his shoes; my father was absent most of my teenage years.

I didn't understand what was happening early on, but I soon realized that choices carried consequences, both good and bad. I realized I was angry with him because he'd left me and missed all the things going on in my life.

Let It Go

I attended a spring revival a few months after my grandfather passed. A prophet of God was the evangelist for the week. I decided to attend because I'd been emotional about my grandfather all week long. When I got there, the evangelist opened the doors of the church and beckoned for everyone dealing with numerous ailments and issues to come to the altar.

I didn't know her, she didn't know me. When she saw I had tears in my eyes, she asked me when I'd last spoken with my father. When I answered her, she said, "Let him go and forgive him."

She told me I had to free myself from the burden and stop blaming myself for his absence. I had to release the anger I had towards him because he wasn't there for me.

She and the other clergymen began to pray, proclaiming that there was nothing like the love of a father. I went down, and basked in God's presence that was in the house.

That night I was released and lost my anger towards my father. I forgave him, and I felt new, relieved and restored from what I had always thought was a loss.

Soon after, I began to pray for my father frequently. I prayed that he would be sustained while away, and that he would know that God was still who He said He was, even in this situation.

Eventually, my dad and I started to write to each other. From there, we moved on to phone calls. We established a one-on-one relationship, and even though he was not there with me physically, he assured me he was proud of me.

In His time

Years went by, and I was still praying for him. Being able to talk to him and know he was doing well soothed my heart. I prayed that God would bring him home in His timing. I prayed for the atmosphere he would be in when he came back. I was the oldest son, and I knew I had to be an example for my younger siblings.

In 2018, God answered prayer, and my dad made it home. The joy I felt from him just being at home is like no other. Our relationship is pretty good, even though it's still being mended. I'm forever grateful that I was able to get past my anger and build a relationship with him.

Xaviar Jackson

Never resent your parents, they've done the best they could. Even bad situations may have come about just because they were only trying to provide for their family. Love them — you are a part of them, and you are here because of them!

Finding Contentment

Being content is being satisfied with how things are at the present moment. I thought I was content, but I actually wasn't. After not being able to advance to the next semester of school, I came home and looked for a job. I ended up returning to a job I'd had before leaving to go to school.

Hear me clearly people. There is a blessing in being able to return to a place when you leave the right way. You cannot be so prideful that you allow yourself to miss what will soon usher you into the next phase.

My work hours were good starting out, but things began to decline as time went by. I took a leap of faith, and landed another job in the healthcare field. I was so focused on making money at this time in my life, I would literally take any job just to say I had full-time employment. I was dependent on the money, not the creator of the money. I had to realize that God would supply my every need.

I began to tithe consistently and God showed up every time. This principle will have you to never lack in any area of your life. Remember that your gift will make room for you. You're not just working to look for payment at the end of each week, you're working to make a difference in the lives you come into contact with each day. Although there is monetary payment, the intangible payment of being appreciated can not be replaced. I learned patience and appreciation for what already is, and took that at face value. Little is made much when God is in it.

God Will Provide

How many times do we try to figure things out for ourselves, when God has already worked them out for us? I truly understand now the reasoning behind the saying: God will provide. If you do your part, from a sincere place in your heart, God will in turn bless you, the cheerful giver.

Blessings don't always come from those you already know, they can come from strangers too. God has to sometimes put you in a new and unfamiliar place in order to give you an unexpected blessing with no name attached to it. When He does this for us, He and only He should get the glory.

With all you do, do it in an upright fashion and from the heart. If you do this, God will bless the very path your feet tread upon. It's a process, but we must learn to let God be God. Trust in His word, and look for Him to do just what He said He would. He will provide for you!

For years I heard people say how good God was. I often wondered about this goodness, and would only repeat the saying because I'd heard others say it. He proved Himself to me and placed it on the heart of someone else to bless me.

In this instant, I knew God to be a provider of all my needs, just as He mentions in scripture.

Remember, he didn't call us to live a perfect life. He wants us to live a lifestyle that is holy and pleasing to Him. Always be mindful of how you treat others because help most times doesn't have a name. Taking your hands off the situation and telling God you can't handle it gives Him room to work.

Sabotage doesn't always come
from others plotting against you or what they
think they know on you.
It sometimes comes from speaking prematurely on things and ideas you have,
but you were not mindful of who you said it to.

Everything He Does is on Time

How does it feel to literally be sat down for a season? I'm glad you asked. It doesn't feel good at all, but it's not until you're almost up again that you figure out why it had to be.

There were so many times I wanted things quick and at the snap of a finger. I never wanted to wait for anything. I'm reminded of the scripture that tells us to be anxious about nothing, but by prayer and supplication make your request known unto God. I had to realize that the God I serve doesn't work inside of time, but everything He does is on time.

My down time was used to get over myself, re-evaluate and re-strategize my plan. As I stated earlier, I had to let God just be God. He had every aspect of my life under control, but I didn't give Him thanks and honor for doing so.

I had exactly a year of down time between my college debut and April 2020. All was not lost during this time. I was continuing to prosper as God desired me to, and life was actually good. I'm grateful and appreciative of how my "breezeway" experience panned out.

What I learned from this experience was I needed to keep the main thing the main thing. If we want to see true change come about, we must be open and honest about how things have impacted us, whether good or bad. We must deliver the message of God in a way that will meet people right where they are. In doing so, you become relative.

Never give up

If you desire to achieve a certain goal in life, never give up on it. It may take years to build upon it, but never stop setting the stones. Your path is uniquely designed just for you, and no one can hinder the promise that God made you. Know wholeheartedly, you are very valuable to the world we live in and what you have to offer is someone's answer to a dream that has not yet been discovered. Keep your momentum through the ups and downs, the quiet times and rough times, and don't stop striving for greater achievement when you arrive at the place you want to be.

You're gonna have to learn that for God to do some things for you fully, you MUST guard those dreams, visions and what He's spoken to you as if your life depends on it!

Final Words from the Author

We meet again. It is my earnest prayer that after reading this book you are motivated to better yourself. It is my desire to be of help and inspiration to everyone I come into contact with.

I believe that real life stories with real reactions bring about real change, and that is why I chose to tell you my story. I want you to know that you should never be ashamed of the path you find yourself taking to get to where God wants you to be. Don't be afraid to tell *your* story, because someone's life might be changed or even saved by hearing it.

Remember, we are one people with many differences, but we have the same goals in mind. May Peace, prosperity and hope be yours. I pray that you too my friend, make it, because I did.

Xaviar D. Jackson

When you become secure in God,
every little wind that blows in your direction
won't cause you to waver!
Are you devoting your trust and confidence to
man, or to the One who made man?

www.ingramcontent.com/pod-product-compliance
Lightning Source LLC
Chambersburg PA
CBHW041132110526
44592CB00020B/2786